ALICE'S CAT

Alice's Cat

ANNE GRIMES

PETERLOO POETS

First published in 2003
by Peterloo Poets
The Old Chapel, Sand Lane, Calstock, Cornwall PL18 9QX, U.K.

**A catalogue record for this book is available
from the British Library**

ISBN   1-904324-09-6

Printed in Great Britain by
Antony Rowe Ltd, Chippenham, Wilts.

ACKNOWLEDGEMENTS

Acknowledgements are due to the editors of the following publications in which many of the poems in this collection first appeared:

Borderlines, Envoi, The Interpreter's House, New Prospects, New Welsh Review, Poetry Wales, Poems from Aberystwyth, She, Welsh National Trust Magazine, Wilfred Owen Newsletter.

Contents

Alice's Cat

New Year's Eve 1990

It began well didn't it, all that euphoria
in Europe, but in the spring an old woman died.
Now a cat dwindles with the year,
an unnamed monster gnawing inside.

Pain is borne with dignity in both cases.
The reek of faeces and urine
does not detract from this. Luminous
eyes implore me to do what I can

which is not much. I change soiled bedding,
speak comforting words I do not believe,
wash, brush, fluff and powder
in a futile effort to deceive

myself. Never one for much touching, now
she grasps my hands,
I was going to say,
as though her life depends

on it. One night I get into her bed.
She is restless. I try to calm
her. She holds me and talks of Dad.
I am bad-tempered, as I always seem

when woken in the middle of the night.
She understands. It is how I am.
When I touch my skeletal cat
he purrs though he can no longer stand

as if flesh will dematerialise
at the approach of death,
leaving only these green burning eyes,
like Alice's cat, to disappear on a breath.

Killing Time

By the mart steps in the main square
girls of thirteen, fourteen
giggle in groups, wait to be seen,
flick and toss their mermaid hair,

flaunt their saunter, prink and pause,
catwalk past in the latest gear,
cut-off tops the thing this year
on midriffs frail as drinking straws

while boys with empty eyes
and nothing else to do
drive round and round the one-way
dragging on fags, their lives

on a tread-wheel, purposeless
as riders on a wall of death.
Sometimes four together,
cabined, they pass and pass.

Traffic lights loom through diesel air.
Arthritic sigh from an artic's brakes.
At the thump, thump of a megawatt bass
a girl near the kerb may fold to a car.

Over the estuary a flare of sunset.
The passenger outlines her lips with a slash,
scarlet on white. The gash
is shocking, a slick of blood on concrete.

Starlings

They congregate at dusk these autumn evenings
where two roads meet, on a patch of dusty grass.
Greenish-black, sinister in the half-light
they group and regroup, a fluid mass

which rises and falls, shifts and lifts
amorphous to a billowing edge
whose tentacles shadow the wind,
tattered polythene on silage.

For a moment chatter becomes a roar,
a turned up radio off-station,
or a loose squawk escapes
and passers-by feel consternation

as darkness thickens. Is there a threat?
One of them elbows me off the path.
In his anorak, a six-pack bought
with his giro from the all-night mart

which is the logic of their location,
he looks harmless enough. Opportunist,
head cocked, alert for danger or fun,
he lives in the present, an existentialist

with a brief past, and an uncertain future.
Seeking safety in numbers he hangs around,
foregathers with mates like birds on a wire
over there by the bus stop on the edge of town.

Funeral Bird

In Turkey, prized for their plumage,
the greenish iridescence of an oil-slick,
here they are given a poor press.
But I appreciate the way they stick
it out when the year is darkest.
Stencilled trees on a blank sky
are suddenly hung with fruit, a harvest
of birds. Then, whoosh, away they fly,
a twirled cloak singed with fire
from the sun's last rays. Or, massed crotchets,
they roost along a telephone wire,
notes for compline on a manuscript.

I sometimes make people into birds.
With her enquiring eye, her dark wing
of hair, her walk a purposeful tread
in old age, I see her as a starling.
She'd chirrup thoughts as they arrived,
filling my father's friendly silence.
"That girl never stops," a tired
teacher had said of her once.
At her funeral, through every prayer and hymn,
a starling jabbered high up in the roof,
flapped into sorrow's private room.
Its familiar chatter lifted grief.

From a Supermarket in Barmouth

Today clouds bruise the summit,
monochrome aquatint. Rain-shafts
slant across the bay. A summer boat

tugs at its moorings clinking sadly.
In the car-park shoppers in anoraks try
to make haste. Awkwardly

they struggle with trolleys whose wheels seem
willfully biased. Two young men in the cream
of youth, young trees, shrug off the storm,

one a dark poplar,
the other burnished beech, hair
marigold-bright in darkening air.

I see then as Arthur's men tilting lances,
spurred on by challenges,
flutters of favour, chances

life hurls them. Now, each pushes a pram
towards a seat for the elderly. Slumped,
they rock their sons with a dumb

tenderness. It's the same each day.
Redundant heroes staring into space
where there are no dragons to slay.

Big Issue

In this sodden summer, a day of heat.
Glitter of sun on the glass of shops,
a flurry of gulls over roof-tops
as tourists file from station to beach

over the crossing there by the lights
where the magazine-seller always stands.
He props up the bins with a brotherhood of friends,
while a scrawny girl with hennaed plaits

hauls at the string of her questing dog,
offers her baby her fag-end to maul.
"Big Issue, Big Issue" the listless call.
Yards off, sprawled like a log

the body of a youth on the burning path.
He's there a long time. No-one stops.
The ants divide as if for a rock,
then reform their ranks. The harsh

sun beats down. What's it about?
Is he drunk, drugged, is it his heart?
Only one Samaritan leans to find out.
The boy sits up. He begins to shout,

to wave his arms. People stop and stare
"What's it to you. What you looking at?"
Concern by the bins. "He mustn't do that.
He'll be sectioned." They've been there.

A wailing ambulance causes a stir.
The stretcher slides in sweet as a drawer.
As the doors shut on the small sad drama
the insects choreograph themselves once more.
The seller resumes his sibilant coo,
"Big Issue. Big Issue, Big Issue."

Kay, the Lost Boy

The thrum of Canada geese as they shoulder
a looking-glass into a feathered sky.
It is a dark glass whose surface,
crazed and clouded, reflects only evil things.
Too heavy, it trembles, topples to earth,
shivers into splinters of ice.
One lodged in the heart will freeze it.

Squalls over the Mersey.
Liverpool's towers wavery through rain.
I was that boy by the ship's rail
shivering to its engine's judder.
Distant, the grey of a heaped sea.
"Care of Christian Brothers Montreal".
I knew about "care". The world held no comfort.
Tears and rain mingled
for my brother on another ship to Australia.
When I asked to go with him
they said they'd filled the quota.

I look into the eyes of my captor;
they are shards of crystal.
If I touch my own they are stone.
The blue of this north light
is the colour of cold.
It illumines a white corridor,
shines on a stained glass window,
on the face of a cruel Christ.
No tears fall here, only hailstones
which lash a skin numb as the soul.
There is no future, no past.

But in my dreams a woman
with dark war-styled hair

leans over a boy in bed,
touches his face, smoothes his pillow.
There is a vase of roses warm as blood
whose glass, cut into facets,
reflects him back to a frozen dawn.

For the hundreds of 'orphans' sent to Canada and Australia after the war.

Braking

These are the freedom riders.
Anoymous in leathers and helmets,
astride their machines like knights of old
they flaunt machismo.
Crouched over handlebars, steel thighs flexed,
they lean at impossible angles,
test the road with the skim of a knee,
measure the margins of danger.
Using wind-drag for braking
they spin in and out of traffic
past cars sedate with luggage,
vanish through heat-haze in the blink of an eye

this first afternoon of real summer
when the sun's spot strobes through trees
and my car thumps to a disco beat.
People are out and about
turning like flowers to the light.
Then, as if someone pressed pause,
a scene of awful stasis.
At a cross-roads three cars crushed.
Figures are statues, stone from shock.
Wheels spin on the skewed bike.
I shall not forget the red and white boots
of the boy on the grass whose stillness stops the heart.

Writing on the Wall

"Don't forget your games skirt,
your father's waiting."
She bundles up her cloud of hair,
skips to the family Astra by the kerb.
He smiles at her. She's his delight

There's a road in the warren behind King's Cross
where arches gulp what light there is
and station ramparts scarp each side
grim as the walls of Pentonville within the mile.
"This used to be our neck of the woods,"
we murmur thinking of trees we've left behind,
that place of daffodils where spring already
stirs beneath a frozen skin.
Here all that stirs is traffic, endless thrust of cars.
There are no woods, no grass,
no window even to break the sooty brick.
Only scrawled chalk messages
of long forgotten causes celèbres.
GEORGE DAVIS IS INNOCENT.
THE D.P.P. CRAWLED HERE.

They come out after dark into a neon gloom,
blank as parking metres along the barren street.
Some in thrall to heroin or pimp,
turn their faces in a rictus of allure.
One scarcely out of childhood,
plump and plain in a parody of uniform,
white school shirt and navy micro skirt
drags on a fag, runs fingers through her spiky hair.
As she leans toward a loitering saloon
there's a glimpse of hockey thigh,
dimpled, purplish in the whipping wind.
Headlamps flash blood letters on a bridge.

The spray-can philosopher. He was here.
DO NOT ADJUST YOUR MINDS.
THERE'S A FAULT IN REALITY.

In an Islington Garden

An evening of unusual warmth
stored in these old walls.
Three blackbirds squabble on the lawn
while a tortoise precisions his feet
with interminable slowness
towards a lettuce leaf.
Lights in the back of the square
gleam through a bonfired dusk.
A dog barks up the street.
Somewhere a party spills into the night

Two people face each other over a table.
They are drinking too quickly.
After all these years he's changed little,
hair still brown, face tanned by Californian sun.
In that last letter he had said,
"To part would be like losing a limb
or declaring ourselves dead".
Her scars are not angry now;
the tissue has whitened, hardened,
but she remembers the pain, tests for it
as one might probe an ulcered tooth.
She makes a joke, her laugh brittle.
He looks puzzled, hurt.
This is not how he remembers her.

The scent of a climbing rose
wreathes them where they sit
and as he leans to fill her glass
suddenly she recalls the smell of his skin.

Tokens

The smiles she hangs about the house
no longer catch his eye.
The face he'd pore on like a favourite poem
gathers dust on the shelf unread.
And the love she lays out on the bed,
folded and fresh the way he likes,
he does not bother to put on.

The Green Dress

A child's hand creeps up
fingers the rivered silk-flow of a dress.

On her side-board one photograph,
a wartime bride, wide-shouldered,
hair rolled, hat a tipped plate,
Sid self-conscious in his suit.
For years her routine set
as her appointed hair,
her clothes pressed and tailored.
She has kept all her surfaces immaculate.

When did we notice a change?
A film of dust, stray wisp of hair.
The obsessions; "I just wanted
to trail my fingers in her watery dress.
They said, 'Don't be so personal.'
It made me cry"
She is beginning to lose her edges.
An ice sculpture slides towards melt.

Flashes of perception, blue eyes direct.
"I think I'm going mad."
She scrabbles in her handbag
as a dog scratches earth for a bone
and looks at us fiercely:
"They said I was being personal.
I was only stroking the satin
of her rippling jade-green dress."

Poacher

That bend in the river where cattle drink
and pebbles pile to a miniature beach,
where a fallen tree, almost a bridge,
traps flotsam in its branches
I once saw a rat-corpse, blown as a foot-ball.
The place I always think I sense otters,
a slither of shadows behind my eyes.
That's where I saw, propped against a stump,
three gaffes, sinister crooks,
the cruel tools of a craft as old as time.

The night is muffle-dark. No moon.
Cocooned in my warm house
I imagine them menacing up-river,
their flashlights winking. A cold blast
from an opening door startles me.
He hands me a sewin the weight of a baby
huge with roe never now to be spawned,
as difficult to grasp as lost soap,
scarcely dead, scales opaline as moonlight,
the dull gleam of a sightless eye.

I dare not refuse, steel myself,
sort from the drawer my sharpest knife.
As I cut off the head the great muscle jerks.
I slit the stomach as an angler taught me,
expose flesh rosy as sunrise,
as eggs spill to a pile of fairy gold.
I scrape the backbone where the skin is black
and all is done. I mourn
a death, not one but many,
the glint of a thousand sickle moons unrisen.

The Cicada Tree

Provence 1991

After that spiralling first-gear climb
amid cicada-crackle
the dark interior of the house welcomes
from noon-white heat with Vivaldi's cool cascade.
Look down on the scorched plain mapped below.
Patched fields, striped, dotted
with terracotta like the background
to one of those mediaeval paintings
where a peasant in red tights pushes
a harrow against a line of trees.
Swathes of sunflowers echo hills' raked ochre.
Nearer, a haze of lavender
where small blue butterflies, trembling
flowerheads which have slipped their stalks,
hover in hot air.

And Gloria of the gleaming Jag,
mugged by Arabs in Avignon,
passport, money, all lost,
tells and retells the story
in a relentless Nebraska drawl,
traces of cheer-leader lingering
on her petulant fifyish face,
needing to boast, her house in Belgravia,
the gardener, the dog-walker.
I hear her on the phone in the hall.
She hectors her husband, wasting,
we learn later of slow disease.
Today's her birthday, celebrated alone.

Outside in the glare of the sun
an olive-tree's a Tower of Babel,

the region's telephone exchange you said.
Sometimes this nerve centre is strangely silent.
Now it explodes in a tangle of sound,
getting our wires all crossed

'Pastel Portraits While You Wait'

Hays Wharf 1998

Monty Gottlieb? Can it be?
Silvered now beneath his artist's hat.
I remember a younger man, his tufted eyebrows,
foxy hair already slipping on his scalp.
A Mayfair furrier. Those square hands
fashioned coats for the pampered.
On his shop a blue and white plaque
told the world that Blake had lived there once,
apt setting for his blend of flair and acumen.

I recall the four of us, two couples
laughing into the wind at Burling Gap
while he hectored oblivious sea-gulls
and the afternoon bled
into evening over a minky sea.
Monty in casual wear. No style at all.
A short-sleeved shirt, arms wiry with copper,
and one of those sleeveless fair-isles
which sometimes fail a comeback.

Weekends we'd stay in the empty flat
above the shop. Tipsying in after a party
by a side-door in the small hours,
we'd sense the sable silkiness of coats
swaying on their hangers in the dark.
Wake to mote-filled sun-shine
burnishing the wormy wood of wall and floor,
the elusive presence of a visionary
like smoke from a snuffed-out candle.

Sunday. Dawn in the West End.
Stillness. A hush of traffic. Almost no people.
Only a few all-nighters in evening-dress,

an early riser scurrying for a paper.
Long ago we moved to new loves, other lives.
Furriers defunct as miners now,
denied the comfort of the higher ground.
Memory curls over a vanished world
but an island rises through the mist.

I touch his arm 'Monty?'

Kate

"She loved the sun," someone muttered
out of the afternoon dark
as we, a straggle of crows, buffeted
by rain and the January gale,
forced our way through rows of "Here Lies",
our umbrellas spoked inside out
like the wings of nailed birds.

No hint of her in the gloom
of the small church. She'd have hated it,
except perhaps for the pew of young constables.
Was it her string of motoring offences
or some dodgy antique brought them here,
so scrubbed, so short-back-and sides?
She'd have liked that.

Afterwards by the waterlogged hole
A huddle of mourners strained to listen
while the priest, his skirts flapping,
intoned "Dust to Dust". "Mud to Mud" more like,
while dun-coloured grave-diggers
lurked behind a line of yews.
Pure Hamlet.

I prefer to remember her
sitting on a stool outside her shop,
that den of rainbows,
scantily clad to catch the sun,
her hair changing from mahogany to pink
over the years, her glorious boobs
the patina of saddle-leather.

Sisters of Charity

These days nuns in mufti pale
into the crowd. I miss the mysterious
swish of habit, the drape of a veil,
their vestal difference from us.
Now, like dowdy librarians,
in grey, black, brown or navy-blue,
buttoned in good Liberty linen,
they seem uncertain how far to go.
Yesterday on the bank a glamour
of snowdrops genuflecting in the sun,
white wimples freshly goffered.
I remembered a convent garden, nuns
taking the air, their coifs' wings
lifted by a lenten wind.

Grandmother's Footsteps

A wax of ice has sealed the pond's preserve
and the stream has swirled a sculpture at its edge.
Spring hesitates, keeps in reserve
the warmth we crave. Huddled by the hedge
snowdrops are merely slips of grass, milk tips,
their bells unpealed. This St David's Day
will fanfare no saffron. The season creeps,
a tantalizing game that children play,
forward then back, intrepid sun
scared off by sudden squalls. Yet all's not lost
for cloud and wind throw benison
of light on here a field or there a mountain crest.
Puddles hold the image of a fiery eye
and catkins shower against a sloe-dark sky.

Foxgloves

Importuning, honeysuckle,
dog-rose's glimpse of flesh,
flaunt sex from the hedge.
Musk of meadowsweet
remembers past summers
as crushed grass exhales
where lately lovers lay as one.
Foxgloves penetrate memory
with a stab of desire.
Digitalis Purpurea:
Stimulant for a flagging heart.

Dog-days

Birds are silent under Sirius. The year
sinks into doldrums. August yawns,
an unstitched gash in unwholesome air
electric with a migraine charge of storms.
Blow-flies whine, torment the ears
of horses, which shake their heads, swish their tails
in irritation. Energy droops. The body yearns
for rain. Yet when at last it falls
its tepid splats bring no relief.
Lightning's knives flick out to wound
a world at bay. I remember strange
superstitions, an old belief:
"In these dog-days no scars will mend",
and I long for autumn with its chance for change.

Suburban Summers

How they yawned before us.
We ached for romance in tree-lined streets
empty of men from nine to six
when breadwinners, like children released from school,
would twirl their umbrellas.
Left with the very young napping in prams
or the very old snoozing in sunshine,
we confronted vast vistas of time.

Games of tennis in the park
where we yearned for bronzed glamour.
Only grey men trailing dogs on leads,
a cormorant keeper stabbing at litter.
Women in panamas heaved
huge bottoms to the knock, knock of bowls.
Gardens echoed to the rattle
of those single boxless mowers, ratchet, ratchet.

Back home along pavements spiced with privet.
We ironed layers of petticoats,
frizzled our fringes with home perms,
nicked Dad's razor so our legs
bled hollyhocks of cotton-wool.
Half blinded by fake lashes
we practiced sexy poses in the glass
while we waited for Real Life to begin.

The past like an old black and white movie
unreels our former selves, familiar
but dated now as roll-ons or strapless bras.
Giggling in the darkness of the cinema

we slurped orange-juice through bent straws,
ogled boys in the front row,
fidgeted through episodes of "Look at Life",
impatient for the start of the big picture.

Dawn

Last night a whorled thumb-print
on the forecast map
witnessed the weather's change of heart.

These days I wake early,
surprised this morning by an absence of water.
No scatter of rain on skylight or tile;

only dew on glass like a first film of frost
screens the slide into autumn.
I can hear in the half dark

two late owls halloo the day
and, where a current splices beyond rocks,
a key-change in the stream's continuo.

A distant tractor clanks and drones
back and forth, back and forth,
husbanding daylight, a last cut of hay

Sun tapers the hillside,
swings a thurible of mist
and islanded trees rise like worshippers
whispering their hour.

Fall

This year, when birds
delay their take-off,
unwilling to leave the party,
chattering in knots, clinging

to the fringes of the light,
summer lingers her gold,
keeps at bay
the encroaching grey.

Autumn gluts gorgeous.
A gift of damsons,
anthracite
glistening blue-maroon.

How to preserve their bloom
before it furs and prunes?
Each fruit enfolds a stone,
flesh liquefying

as the skin splits.
Tiny animal,
moly,
like the headless mice

my cat drops
on the threshold
where my bare feet pad
in cold half light.

To tread on a damson
in the darkness
of the apple-store
is to feel a yielding

a spurt of blood.
Both our skeletons
beneath the skin.

Trapped

Between stream and hill the track is blocked,
mud and rocks heaped up. There's no way through.
Our house becomes an island now, landlocked,
a pebble in a globe of green and blue.

Mud and rocks heaped up. There's no way through.
The mind like a top spins round and round,
or a pebble in a globe of green and blue.
We lurk in our lair like foxes gone to ground.

The mind like a top spins round and round,
We pace the floor as prisoners in a cell,
lurk in our lair like foxes gone to ground.
'Huis Clos' Sartre called it. Is this hell?

We pace the floor as prisoners in a cell.
Small hours interrogate with torturer's light.
'Huis Clos' Sartre called it. Is this hell?
This blurring of the line from day to night.

Small hours interrogate with torturer's light.
Our house becomes an island now, landlocked
with a blurring of the line from day to night,
now that between stream and hill the track is blocked.

Waiting

Now is the valley's darkest time,
a time for tunnelling in, for hunkering down,
when parchment sky's cross-hatched by slats of rain
and trees' veined shapes are etched in monochrome.
October bronze has turned has turned to dun
on Rhiwbren's hill. Bracken sags to rust
through morning dank of mist or mould of frost,
while sombre ranks of woods obscure the sun.
Sap sinks, twigs brittle and pared
as your frail bones in your hospital bed.
With your hair on end, your bare chest wired
exposed and helpless as a baby bird.
So long you've waited for the surgeon's art
to uncongeal the blood and heal the heart.

Lost Jewels

On a sky-light's dark square
an oval moon,
flattened like the last pearl
on a necklace trailing from the shelf.
I love the milky opacity of pearls,
like drops of semen, needing
flesh to kindle them to life,
the sappy green of jade.

"See," said the Chinese girl, cupping
my jade in her hand,
"look how the colour deepens."
Jade and pearl, precious as snowdrops.
Sometimes now I dream of jewels
and when I dream I dream of loss.
I see only clouds moving against an oyster sky
and the green earth fading.

Eclipse of the Moon

Where the leat widens
into a pond's eye
the water is black but clear.
Two goldfish the boy
poured from polythene
play dead, peach slices
at the bottom of a dish,
or splinter the dark with light.

At this winter season
the woods are feathery
brushed with colour.
Branches' moving patterns
meet their doppelgangers
at the water's edge
where another forest begins.
Clouds scud and drift.

This is the border of difference
between waking and sleep.
Dreams mirror a world
bent from day's norm
by the mind's refraction.
Last night, riding a nightmare,
I saw a blood-rimmed moon
stare at her own drowned face.

Lost Child

Reflected in the cubicle mirror
her hospital gown's an iceberg.

Hope's last snipped thread
spins her back to the moon.

Far away in a cold cavern
an anchoress queen drums icicle fingers.

Hers the realm of endless light,
Aurora Borealis beaming

the always blue of attrition.
Lonely Queen of the Snowbees

on her glass throne
where blizzards of unborn children swarm

she gazes into the sea-eyes of Kay,
her captive, her changeling.

Hailstones melt on her face.
She dreads these tears for they are warm

and where they fall red roses spring.
Whose blood is this which seeps into the snow?

Hour of the Wolf

Wakefulness is white,
a half remembered face
bobbing on a crowd-wave
or the March moon's death-mask
pressed against the pane.

Martinet,
she choreographs stars,
pieces of silver. Pleiades leap
like pound-signs on a till,
fiscal fish.

Crouched in corners
deserted dolls disjoint,
seize the dozes and dance
like toys in the old stories.
Close your eyes and you'll miss them.

Through the forests of the ear
dream-wolves are padding
nearer-nearer.
Outside a solitary owl calls
lonely as an unanswered phone.

Persephone

Loiters among shadows
in subway corridors.
A rank breeze harries litter;
it skirls at her feet where

bundles of rags stir
in the foetid air.
'Homeless' beats in her brain
to the roar of a train

always a tunnel away.
Happiness a yesterday
whose flashbacks tantalize
and flicker over frozen eyes.

On a moving staircase
she scans without interest
anonymous shapes which ascend
towards light as she descends.

One face, asterisked, seems
familiar. A smile gleams
in the tenebrous space
between them, then fades

as they pass. She recalls another face,
two women walking by water in a place
where that year daffodils were early,
and sun splashed fields with colour.

Now on the river's bank
a red bull dips his head to drink.
His sanguine shade propitiates
the dark where memory waits.

Persephone's Return

Indigo night. Wakened by owls. They call
to each other out of a feathered dark,
as we, your friends, longing to lure you back,
hallooed the purple labyrinths of Pluto's hall
and found you changed. You did not recognize us,
your smile pasted. We watched your self-hood ebb
to a shrunken spider in a stifling web.
Now you are transformed. Joyous
we see you standing haloed in the moist
entrance to the cave behind the waterfall
where last autumn we found your girdle loosed.
Like Naiads, cuckoo-flowers trawl
their toes, daffodils shimmy to the east,
and the bulb of your being leaps to spring's call.

Further Education

Late almost always their heads peer
around the door, sporadic
as the lecture-room heater

which coughs out chalky air.
Young women, chickens from the coop,
enquire the day. Their

bruised eyes reveal the fatigue
of broken nights, demanding partners,
babies; nerves taut from the cross-tug.

I can see Chloe in the car-park.
Released, she flings back mermaid hair.
It fountains raindrops over her anorak.

Nearly all of them wear jeans,
the universal uniform. Clack, clack
along the corridor. Only Kathleen's

high heels conform to a more dated mode,
low neck, tight skirt, blonde hair.
She has settled her husband on his commode,

telephone to hand, thermos, cigarettes.
Does he scent a secret affair?
It is passion but not what he suspects.

Today we are reading Heaney.
suddenly the rhymes come alive
as Anne, Protestant from Ballymeena

uncovers the significance of "cache",
exposes her flight from the Troubles.
Last week a current from Sylvia Plath

shocked Sian who hasn't spoken all term
into stuttering speech.
She confided her own dark time.

Enter Megan. Two tiny children
cling to her legs. It is half-term.
She has nowhere to leave them

and bribes them on to stools with crayons,
their eyes huge as we discuss
"Middlemarch". Casaubon's

proposal. Jane, married to an ex-
R.A.F. type 60+ offers up
her own life. Not much sex

she says. I am the teacher taught.
Their faces open like petals.
Tiredness falls away as they contemplate

problems not their own. While
they strive to push out boundaries
the two children, a boy and a girl,

crouch over colouring-books. Their legs twine
round struts of the stool, tongues thrust out
in their efforts not to go over the line.

February, Jamie and Sylvia Plath

Awkward, crouched over the page,
he writes with the back-to-front fist
of the left-handed, frowns over Sylvia Plath.
Yesterday at karate he said he fought
the whole club one by one. His skin shines,
hair dense and matt as a dog's fur.
What can he know of finger-tip despair
or *cold homicides* which *weld like plums?*
"Like, there was this party, see.
A plum-pie left in the microwave.
No way could we scrape it off".
Beyond the plate-glass of the Portacabin
as ecstasy of blue dims suddenly.
Trees fling themselves
back and forth, wringing their hands.
Lightning shocks convulse in thunder.
The afternoon sags. Deep indigo.

Auden Reading

His face a mud-flat
crazed by drought. Iguana eyes
regard us unblinking.
Dry scales sufflate.
We expect a flick of the tongue,
not that old man's cardigan,
frayed string of hair, huge feet
zipped into felt slippers
shuffling beneath the table.

Or has memory superimposed
a biographical detail
like his insistence on time-keeping,
his habit of retiring early
in other people's houses,
hauling the carpet over his bed
to keep terror at bay:
that *watcher in the shadows*
who coughs when we would kiss.

The day of his death.
Through a side window
London light illumines
his umber profile.
The day of his death.
His belfry baritone
extols the memory of Yeats.
the day of his death
was a dark, cold day.

Graham Sutherland at Picton Castle

A castle guardant, grey
on cloth of gold and green,
scarfed by a favour of aconites
blue as distance.
In a tang of undergrowth each tree
the spoil of sprig's grand tour,
immigrants with impeccable connections.
Where a brown stream rusts its pebbles
Pembrokeshire light sharpens
leaves to acid yellow, bitter lime.
Thorns twist awkwardly,
their black barbs sinister

jag paintings in the gallery
where recognition shivers as in dream,
everything familiar yet different.
The same heraldic colours:
peacock, blood and gold
kaleidoscope, shift shape.
From an orange sky an brown sun
emblazons a great trunk
whose boa-constrictor root
writhes, convolutes; subsides
to a heap of rotting anchor chain
through the alchemy of art.

Audition

I can hear those driven feet
unobserved in a dressing-room
just off Oxford Street,

and see through the open door
to a studio's mirrored vista one black dancer
pirouette solemnly to his own reflection.

Here, Jeyes Fluid, hair-spray, fail to mask
the cloy of female flesh, damp concrete,
yesterday's stale sweat.

Aspirants prepare. Their trained bodies
fall into attitudes unself-consciously.
Plié to pick up a shoe exposes

glimpses of pubic hair flattened by nylon,
a dangling tampon string,
rhizomed toes.

An arm raised with hair-brush reveals
breasts fragile as flowers
on their tensile stem.

They limber in lycra,
flash kingfisher colour,
brief gleam of damsel flies.

Intent, set out pins and combs,
stare into glass like cats into a pond,
calculating their chances.

Outside it begins to rain. I hear its insistent beat,
the tap, tap, tap, ...tap, tappety tap
of forty driven feet.

A Time to Dance

Remembrance Day. 1994

Take it from the top.
Dance to the heart's pulse
and-a-one and-a-two.
Smile, it may never happen,
not to anyone we know.

Remember his dancer's body
taut in black leather
(exotic in our green valley)
like a dark candle,
the pale flame of face and hair.

Chorus boy on the P&O line
cruising. He'd dim his brightness.
A bushel to shield his father,
his comfortable Swansea mother
who treasured his tales of Acapulco, San Juan,

oblivious of blood-brothers,
brief bar-room encounters
before the ship sailed on.
Would blame themselves maybe.
Flesh of their flesh. Dust of their dust.

Today the band plays.
Old soldiers halt in memory,
a generation untimely reaped.
Dylan has taken off his costume for the last time.
Its scarlet ribbons flutter in the mind
and love lies bleeding.

Dylan died of aids November 1994

Time Please

A sepia scene, lost in the album
of some other family member
the way legacies go.
My mother, born 1906.
ten when she held her pose
for a hooded tripod
back of the Midland Pub Luton

crouched grim as a cannon against a sooty arch
where brown L.M.S.'s pounded north,
screamed over the bridge and down the line,
set glasses trembling in the bar,
caused greenish gas
to dip and flare and forced
a lull in taproom chat.

Held smiles frozen forever.
Camera's sights on the grandfather
I never knew, this his only image.
He stands tall and stout
in shirtsleeves and waistcoat.
Genial, balding, moustached,
filling the landlord's central place.

My grandmother is there too,
leg-of-mutton sleeves, Queen Alexandra hair,
and some soldiers in battledress,
khaki-stiff with blancoed webbing.
They grin with the buoyancy of men who've had a few beers
and have pushed my mother to the front.
I can see her black stockings, her white dress,

the soldier's cap on her long dark hair.
Now she's their mascot.
What are they celebrating? Someone's birthday?
Or a last drink then off to the Front
in that war when townsmen and pals
joined up together, gasped out their lives together
in the stinking mud-holes of the Somme?

Scars

His nose, broken in crashes, nine
so he claimed, collapsed towards its base,
then swelled to a comic tip, the face
of a garden gnome, innocent, malign.
In his Sopwith Pup, fragile as Airfix,
a tiny pilot perched on cushions to scan
the sky for Fokkers, one hand to man
the gun, the other to clutch at joystick's
straw. Against all odds this one survived;
even the earlier mud-blood of the Somme
where he couldn't get a Blighty. Though he tried.
What did he feel, those long years at home?
Was it guilt, or a shameful twinge of pride
he should live when all his friends had died?

His son's scar, visible between neck and vest,
conforms to bullet's ricochet and runs
from wrist to elbow, shoulder to chest.
He was nineteen on D-Day when guns
raked beaches, those evocative titles:
Utah, Omaha, Juno, Gold;
Boys picked off, new-hatched turtles
exposed to deadly strafe from swooping gulls.
How beautiful the names of cruel events:
Passchendale, Ypres, Mons, Verdun.
It is the opal shimmer of decay. A sense
of desolation lingers in the sound.
When he raises his cup you can see the scar,
a livid cicatrice of war.

Stairs

1941. The space under the stairs
our makeshift shelter from the Blitz.
We three children, gas-masks, blankets,
cramped together in stuffy air
for a few nights. But the grown-ups grew bored
waiting for bombs that didn't happen.
Instead we peered through black-out at London,
its sky smouldering, till ordered
back to chilly beds. We were spared,
except for the odd Dornier dumping its load,
too young to comprehend the nightly deaths.
Only, later, I saw bombed roads
houses without fronts. Those stairs.
Wall-paper flapping, pink like shreds of flesh.

Double Summertime

This farmers' friend stretched the day beyond
the children's bedtime. Useless for parents to insist
that night had come when all the evidence belied
their words: the chirruping of birds, that glimpse
of thistle-cloud on blue, intrusive sun
the densest blackout could not exclude.
Once, when sunlight beckoned them on,
they rode their bikes through car-less streets to a wood,
their secret place. Their daytime world had changed;
bright shafts through green entrapping flies
as searchlights beamed on enemy planes
and pinned them to the dark. Westerly, before their eyes
the sunset dimmed, yet, southward London's
skyline flamed. They heard the growl of guns.

Sea

For wartime children holidays were rare
so the sea became myth, a green depth in the mind,
yet sometimes as we rode our bikes where
lanes were dusty with summer and lines
of heat made a watery shimmer, we knew
the sea lay behind the crest of the hill,
there where the road wound upward and the blue
breast of sky leaned nearer. I can still
feel that imagined thrill. Then the let-down
as landlocked fields spread out below.
Now at last the dream is real. I've found
the very road. It runs uphill through
Blaen Pant farm. From there on a clear day
to see the rippling harp of Cardigan Bay.

Turning

Those wartime winters the house was bleak.
Frost etched arctic landscapes inside
each window. Every bed-time we'd
falter upstairs, youngest first, into a dark
deepened by blackout, reaching for the light.
When terror had slipped into its own shadow, heat
was slow to seep from our bodies into icy sheets
stamped with *Utility's* double bite.
For her life was hard. Not enough money
or coupons when fabrics wore out.
Always the burden: *Make Do and Mend.*
When she died, amongst her things a sheet.
recalled her at her Singer turning
sides to middle, end to end.

War Effort

A farm asleep in afternoon sun
sprawled like a hay-maker relaxed
after labour, brick limbs outflung.
On air the drying smell of cow-pats,

hay, a reek from the sties.
They climbed the fence, awkward,
with gas-masks banging their thighs,
the carrier bag between them, into the yard.

No-one about. Sunshine and shadow
sized each other up. Indolent
in a patch of warmth a cat opened
her eyes, then closed them, indifferent.

A world far away from war.
That word frightened them less
than the masks themselves whose odour
sickened, like the dentist.

Childhood cushioned them
yet fear was everywhere. They'd smelled it
rising from lines of labelled children,
rained-soaked, homesick, waiting for a billet.

Bill-boards screamed slogans:
Dig for Victory, Waste Not Want Not.
That was why they'd collected acorns.
This bulging bag their war effort.

Now to leave their offering
at the pig-sty back of the yard.

Tip-toe they peered in
when out of the dark a vast sow reared,

tiny eyed, trailing snot from her jaw,
snout trained on them like an ack-ack gun.
She heaved her tonnage over the half-door
and for the duration blotted out the sun.

Geraniums

Survivors. They straggle out of winter dark;
etiolated stems reach for the light
while brittle branches crack
like the bones of the starved. One bright
bloom lifts it face. A pungency,
spiced, peppery, unlocks lost summers:
terra-cotta pots on a wall in Provence,
a drowned terrace after rain. Remember
that petal pasted on stone, one drop of blood.
A woman's voice. *When we went into Belsen*
six weeks after the Allies had entered,
there was a smell, sweetish, not unpleasant
like crushed geranium. Now to pinch a leaf
is to breathe again that quickening grief.

Thoughts of War

By a sand-pit, Maes Chwarae, Aberaeron,
a sad girl with arab robes on

sits on the roundabout listlessly tilting
her baby, faltering

a lullaby. Breath fumes in cold air.
Proud, with his mother, a boy soldier

parades in winter sunshine, his khaki
as stiff and new as cardboard.

Above the hard collar his school-team face
glows with ignorance,

young brave spoiling to test his manhood.
I remember those others waving shiny-eyed

from the Canberra, the cheering, the euphoria,
remember the day they came back victorious,

some minus limbs, minus skin, minus hair;
and in their scorched eyes despair.

Formation Flying

Swifts with us all summer long;
a pair of them, looping, wheeling,
skimmed the edge of consciousness,

as scarce perceived as swaying trees,
familiar shimmy of fish,
stream's background conversation.

How gracefully that precision pair,
in display formation, dipped and circled
their joyous laps around our lives.

Now autumn menaces. Mist hangs
like mustard-gas over military tents
of spiders bivouacked in grass,

the valley never quieter
than that second before a thunderclap
detonates its terror

and a Tornado, blinking red,
streaks below the hill, banks,
then turns behind the tree-line,

its pilot almost palpable,
male, young, aroused
by this deadly foreplay.

Skin shrinks from flesh.
In a nerve-jangle, heart-lurch,
we wait for the second one pat on his tail.

Clouds muster in the east. Uneasy
we watch, high up, two vapour-trails
scrawl threats across a darkening sky.

Wind-flowers

After Chernobyl

Wood-anemones,
Easter bridesmaids
shiver in a bitter breeze,
bending their heads together.
Blood-tinged petals
pale as skin-flakes
tremble on the wind.

Winds from the east
scatter evil seed
planted in bone
to blanche the blood.
There is a shudder
along the vein as, slowly,
the white blooms multiply.

Boy Soldiers

So many of them trapped in wars
they're too young to understand, old causes
whose roots tangle beyond their short lives,
follow their brothers with clubs and knives,
brandish guns they are scarcely big enough
to hold; ten year olds with kalashnikovs.
They lounge at their posts, drag on cigarettes.
Miniature men with eyes of fanatics.
For the hell of it they spray fusillades
in the air, hurl stones across barricades.
This game is for real, their faces hard,
planed down by war, stick limbs scarred.
Only at night when they collapse in sleep
may childhood curves return, their mouths droop.
Or, sometimes in daylight, caught unawares,
their huge eyes seem to gaze
back beyond the Rubicon they crossed
to throw in their lot with the corps of the lost.

About Suffering

About suffering they were never wrong the old masters. W.H. Auden

We cannot turn away
from this horror in the living-room.
Compelled to watch the dreadful martydom
as the flame-rose opens its petals.

It's not the vast statistics of death
touch us but the isolated image:
a boy falling out of the sky
floor after floor after floor,

a handkerchief fluttered from a melting window,
that girl in the tower
stuttering love into her mobile
seconds before her heart is stopped.

Shrines

On roads this summer such sad nosegays,
ribbons drooping, petals beginning to wilt.
A planted plot the shape of a grave
where skid-marks slew to the accident spot.
How close we steer to the edge of dark,
each of us an eye-blink from the abyss.
These flowers rest here as a mark
of grief from anonymous givers.
The dead live briefly in the public eye
as traffic passes, as traffic passes
before the bundles tatter and die.
That lurch in the gut reminds us
we are insects on a windscreen,
a gambler's throw against a crimsoned sun.

Return

There on the mat after her holiday
a letter everyone dreads.
The words 'slight abnormality'
with a date for further tests.
"It's simply routine," we say
with forced cheerfulness
while an iron-maiden tightens her embrace.

Dark Welsh weather when
we drive to Carmarthen
through mourning hills creped with rain.
The stopping train to Swansea
creaks along interminably,
steaming clothes, stale bodies,
a baby's fretful whine.

We arrive too early
so it's sandwiches at the station,
uncleared ashtrays, tasteless tea.
It must be the day of graduation.
At the next table gowned girls
smoke and giggle over their coffee.
Their laughter taunts anxiety.

Professional smiles at reception.
Deliberate blandness in the decor,
the murmur of strained conversation.
Each side of the desk a door,
both blank, one for 'out', one 'in'.
People peer at them with concern.
Her name's called. She's the first in.

Women who went in after her come out
smiling, their faces freshly ironed.
I stare at my obsolete magazine
feeling a weight beneath my heart.
Now she's the only one left.
I glance at the women behind the desk
their smiles kinder, frighteningly less brisk.

Suddenly she's there. I scan her expression.
"I'm alright, a simple excess of oestrogen
no-one spotted until I saw the surgeon."
We almost dance into the shining street
while Atropos pockets her scissors again,
dazzle at the glory of the light,
the radiance of that wino through the rain.

Pain

I picture him at home in the special chair
we brought at Argos, now the only one
with any comfort. I can see him there
hunched strangely, half kneeling down
at his computer. I register its blip,
and at odd times catch a stifled groan
as neurons twang from spine to hip.
He is an expert now in kinds of pain:
the serpent wriggling along a limb,
the unexpected jab to the quick.
More merciful the far-off crump
of thunder. Worst the electric flick
which leaps from nerve to nerve like light
or fission's annihilating white.

Silver Wedding

Twenty-five years
and the same capricious sun
clicks its shutter
on a group in the pub garden, unchanged,
give or take a partner or two,
yet subtly different
like those computer-aided images
in insurance commercials
showing a couple twenty, thirty years on.
Some guests are missing.
They lie nearby in the churchyard
under ripples of seeded grass.
Only one spry old aunt
holds a key to vanished years
between the two great wars,
the answers to questions
no-one will bother to ask.
With a second glass of champagne
voices and colour begin to rise.
These men, executives with BP, the BBC
are accustomed to being listened to.
Their well-dressed, well-wearing wives
eye them anxiously when they are not looking.
Coronaries and cancer stalk unseen.
As evening draws in
a freakish cloud throws a shadow
on a woman's face, recalling
the pale shy girl she used to be.

Jumping-off

"Hi! Mum!" His voice sun-filled, bright as the day
he walked through the departure-gate
without a backward glance.
"Christmas on the beach. Great!"
Thousands of miles shrink
to a cobalt sky tight over kangaroo sands.

Here a wolf-wind snarls at her door.
Forty days and nights of rain.
The ark of her house shudders in its swell
then grounds itself uneasily.
On the hill black branches heave,
the creaking of ship's timbers.

A river in spate has transformed itself
from summer's drowsy lizard
to this leviathan lashing its tail.
It bounces a brick chimney-stack
as if it were a cardboard-box.
All day she can hear it roar.

She watches the video he's sent,
a world of primary colour
like a corn-flake packet, sky, grass,
yellow of the landing-strip, red flying-gear.
Each creature has an aura in that heat.
Young Elijahs, transfigured, limber for their ascent

heads thrown back, arms outstretched,
cruciform against their partners.
When the may-bug plane takes off
men inside adjust straps and faces.

A nervous joke, a last word.
Then, bound belly to back, they jump,

crane-flies in mid-air,
turning over and over,
faces peeled back in the wind.
For one thousand feet before the spinning earth
presses upwards and the rip-cord must be pulled,
youth's too brief free-fall.

Weekend

Wet wisteria drips from the half door.
Beyond a curtain of Gwen John lace
the vista'd garden. Flower-colours
leach into an intensity of green.

They've driven away. A lowering week-end
Swagged clouds, a hint of headaches.
On the hillside, trees hung motionless
murmuring distant thunder.

No chance for those imagined drinks
under the sun umbrella,
the tinkle of Pimms in the frosted jug
they'd brought me. A couple now.

Difficult to talk alone,
to return to that distant but familiar
childhood when I was a barrier
between him and danger, could stop

him toddling towards a precipice,
splashing into the deepest part of the stream.
I have let go. Only when I see him
do old anxieties surface.

Saturday night, and I'm still foolishly alert
for returning headlights on the bedroom wall.
In dreams, when a child runs
into traffic, I'm unable to move.

Now as I watch, two cats
eye each other warily.
A fat drop hangs in tension.
Thunder growls, an uneasy dog.

Mother and Daughter

She rides the wind
like a kite pulling taut
against the mooring
of my restraining hand.
When a sudden gust
jerks the string
the frantic head
dips and veers
this way and that
desperate to break the thread,
soar up out of sight.
I, grounded today,
cup my hand to shield
the small flame of myself.

City at Night

(Marina Tsvetaeva.) From a literal translation.

I feel the night around me, close, vast
as the sleeping town. I leave the dream-fast
house; my role of daughter, wife, cast
off. There is only night and no past.

From a window somewhere music drifts, borne
on the July wind. It will blow till day's dawn
and sweep a path for me. Oh it will barnstorm
my heart, burst through my breast's thin drum.

I catch gleams from a window. Spilled light
showers a poplar. I hear from a tower's height
a peal of bells and pluck a flower. Pat
on my heels a shadow, a step. They're not

mine. I'm somewhere else. In the dark, streets
are necklaces of light. Night's leaf melts
on the tongue. Release me now from daylight's
bonds. My friends, I am what you dream at nights.

Absence

Some images imprint the mind
and stamp the heart, a pair of child's shoes
sprawled on the stairs, their laces loose,
shucked off in a hurry, one on its side.
Or my father's hat still on his car's rear shelf
six months on, its tweedy shape
holding his essence for a second's leap
of hope, then back to the plateau of grief.
A dusty trainer beneath the bed, where
the hoover does not reach, evokes my son
away in his man's world. How they hurt,
these glimpses. As with a sore
tooth, probing, I imagine you too, gone:
those strewn socks, that abandoned shirt.

Grandma and Cyril

When you mentioned Luton
(Luton meaning Low Town)
I saw my grandmother toiling
on bunioned feet uphill
to her terraced house in High Town.
I could see her small back-room
almost filled by a table laid for tea,
bread-wedges carved frighteningly
against her chest, a Co-op
slab cake from the corner shop.
I hear from her grate a plop of flame,
the tick of the clock in its glass dome
as she listens for the chain clicking
on her son's bike, the last son left living.

Upright on a stiff-backed chair,
hands clasped in her lap, steel hair
piled high, always in a navy-blue gown,
she's a country woman trapped in town.
At ninety she sang an ancient welcome to May
verse after verse, though her memory of yesterday
was hazy. Now her remaining energies centre
on my uncle: that lugubrious bachelor.
She has pressed and brushed his suit
for his one night out with Albert
at a pub whose toilets are *Mermaids, Mariners,*
and where he'll take his pleasures
glumly every Friday of every year.
Two men, not speaking, staring into their beer.

Names

No-one remembers her as a girl.
Only Alfred. Then it clicks.
(so often caught out by the mind's tricks)
Alfred's long dead, and the sunny world
they shared gone too. No-one now to say her
Christian name. Always 'Mum' or 'Granny'.
Never the once familiar 'Annie'.
To punish us God grants our prayer.
A voice, at once patronizing, brisk.
Loud too as if she were deaf or senile.
No respect. 'Annie dear, this is
your day for the chiropodist.'
It's the home's policy. He means well
the nurse. Why can't he call her 'Mrs?'

Ghosts

After my mother died I'd catch sight
of her everywhere, at Tesco's check-out
in front of me, her implacable hat,
her Aquascutum tweed. I'd know the set
of that head, the stance, angle of jaw,
until she turned and I'd see a face
droop with different wrinkles, the flesh more
pale, more red, more plump. Someone else,
not her at all, and I'd snatch my breath
like missing a stair. When I wear the coat
she bought herself the month before her death
I feel I've become my own grey ghost.
Once, as I approached a shop-window pane,
there was my mother peering at me through the rain.

Waiting for a Birth

Left-over Christmas
New Year not yet born.
Grills of sleet imprison us
in a house hunkering in frost.
Blood cools and slows.
We, animals too in hibernation,
snuggle under bed-clothes,
listen to the noises of night:
a fox snuffling the bin,
owl's solo "Nunc Dimittis".

Morning brings birds of day.
Beggars, they jostle for crumbs.
Wind flutters their starved rags,
sprays hail like machine-gun fire
over the blind pond's milky eye.
Cruciform shirts hang stiff on the line.
A time of suspended animation.
We have celebrated a birth,
now we wait for another, ears turned
to the phone's "Magnificat."

Honeymoon

"There's a law against taking a girl into a bean-field."
Evening skims our open car. "Never been repealed.
The musk of its flowers arouses such desire
women fall prey to its languorous power."

Has he made it up? Our marriage only eight hours old.
Around us fields spread groundsheets of gold
as we speed eastward, leaving friends
at a loss what to do with the day's fag-end.

It's June. Sweetness of hay on the air,
dog-roses in the hedge. We go where
the road takes us. Hotels all full
with Newmarket racegoers. A single at the Bull,

extra mattress on the floor hastily improvised,
my hat placed firmly on the bed as befits the bride,
your case on the other. Later we linger over a meal.
A vast bouquet. You must have done the deal

at reception. They're the flowers from the desk.
My tongue savours salmon, moist texture of flesh,
relishing your hands as you pour the wine,
Spilled light on the table, the last rays of sun.